Cake Mix Magic

Publications International, Ltd.
Favorite Brand Name Recipes at www.fbnr.com

Louis Weber, CEO
Publications International, Ltd.
7373 North Cicero Avenue
Lincolnwood, IL 60712

Pictured on the front cover *(clockwise from top left):* Chocolate Peanut Butter Cups *(page 38),* Chocolate Cherry Torte *(page 90),* Chocolate Banana Cake *(page 33)* and Strawberry Vanilla Cake *(page 86).*

Pictured on the back cover *(clockwise from top left):* Cheesecake-Topped Brownies *(page 60),* Individual Cheesecake Cups *(page 76),* Fudgy Ripple Cake *(page 26)* and Chocolate Chip 'n Oatmeal Cookies *(page 56).*

ISBN: 0-7853-5172-8

Manufactured in China.

8 7 6 5 4 3 2 1

Microwave Cooking: Microwave ovens vary in wattage. Use the cooking times as guidelines and check for doneness before adding more time.

Preparation/Cooking Times: Preparation times are based on the approximate amount of time required to assemble the recipe before cooking, baking, chilling or serving. These times include preparation steps such as measuring, chopping and mixing. The fact that some preparations and cooking can be done simultaneously is taken into account. Preparation of optional ingredients and serving suggestions is not included.

Cake Mix Magic

Baking Secrets

The Basics

It doesn't take a magician to make delicious treats! Simply follow these guidelines for successful baking.

- Read the entire recipe before beginning to make sure you have all the necessary ingredients and baking utensils.
- Remove butter, margarine and cream cheese from the refrigerator to soften, if necessary.
- Toast and chop nuts, pare and slice fruit, and melt chocolate before preparing the batter or dough.
- Measure all the ingredients accurately and assemble them in the order they are called for in the recipe.
- Always use the pan size specified in the recipe, and prepare the pan as directed in the recipe.
- When substituting glass bakeware in recipes that call for baking pans, reduce the oven temperature by 25°F.
- Adjust the oven racks and preheat the oven. Check the oven temperature for accuracy with an oven thermometer.

The Perfect Pan

Baking Pan: Metal baking pans are square, rectangular or round, and have straight sides at least 1½ inches high. The most common sizes are 8- and 9-inch square or round; 11×7×2 inches; and 13×9×2 inches. Baking pans (sometimes referred to as cake pans) are designed for cakes and bar cookies. Shiny aluminum pans are ideal for producing a tender, lightly browned cake crust.

Baking Sheet: A baking sheet (often referred to as a cookie sheet) is a flat, rigid sheet of metal on which stiff dough is baked into cookies, rolls, biscuits, etc. It has a low lip on one or more sides for ease in handling; a lip higher than one-half inch interferes with surface browning, especially of cookies. The type of surface also determines the browning characteristics of the baking sheet. Shiny finishes promote even browning. Dark metal baking sheets absorb more heat and can cause food to brown too quickly. Insulated baking sheets have a layer of air sandwiched between two sheets of aluminum which helps to prevent excess browning, but increases baking time. (Some cookie doughs may also spread more on these sheets.) Nonstick finishes minimize sticking and make cleanup easier.

Measuring Magic

Dry Ingredients: Always use standardized measuring spoons and cups. Fill the appropriate measuring spoon or cup to overflowing, and level it off with a metal spatula or the flat edge of a knife.

Liquid Ingredients: Use a standardized glass or plastic measuring cup with a pouring spout and calibrations marked on the side. Place the cup on a flat surface, fill to the desired mark, and check the measurement at eye level.

Charming Classics

Philadelphia® Marble Brownies

1 package (21½ ounces) brownie mix
1 package (8 ounces) PHILADELPHIA® Cream Cheese, softened
⅓ cup sugar
½ teaspoon vanilla
1 egg
1 cup BAKER'S® Semi-Sweet Real Chocolate Chips

PREPARE brownie mix as directed on package. Spread in greased 13×9-inch baking pan.

MIX cream cheese, sugar and vanilla until well blended. Add egg; mix well. Pour over brownie mixture; swirl with knife. Sprinkle with chips.

BAKE at 350°F for 35 to 40 minutes or until cream cheese mixture is lightly browned. Cool in pan on wire rack. Cut into squares. *Makes 24 brownies*

Philadelphia® Marble Brownies

Orange Pecan Gems

1 package DUNCAN HINES® Moist Deluxe® Orange Supreme Cake Mix
1 container (8 ounces) vanilla low fat yogurt
1 egg
2 tablespoons butter or margarine, softened
1 cup finely chopped pecans
1 cup pecan halves

1. Preheat oven to 350°F. Grease cookie sheets.

2. Combine cake mix, yogurt, egg, butter and chopped pecans in large bowl. Beat at low speed with electric mixer until blended. Drop by rounded teaspoonfuls 2 inches apart onto prepared cookie sheets. Press pecan half onto center of each cookie. Bake at 350°F for 11 to 13 minutes or until golden brown. Cool 1 minute on cookie sheets. Remove to cooling racks. Cool completely. Store in airtight container.

Makes 4½ to 5 dozen cookies

Orange Pecan Gems

Easy Carrot Cake

- 1¼ cups MIRACLE WHIP® Salad Dressing
- 1 two-layer yellow cake mix
- 4 eggs
- ¼ cup cold water
- 2 teaspoons ground cinnamon
- 2 cups finely shredded carrots
- ½ cup chopped walnuts
- 1 (16-ounce) container ready-to-spread cream cheese frosting

• **PREHEAT** oven to 350°F.

• **BEAT** salad dressing, cake mix, eggs, water and cinnamon in large bowl with electric mixer at medium speed until well blended. Stir in carrots and walnuts.

• **POUR** batter into lightly greased 13×9-inch baking pan.

• **BAKE** 35 to 40 minutes or until wooden toothpick inserted in center comes out clean. Cool completely. Spread cake with frosting. Garnish as desired.

Makes 12 servings

Prep Time: 15 minutes
Bake Time: 35 minutes

Creamy Lemon Bars

- 1 package (2-layer size) lemon cake mix
- 3 large eggs, divided
- ½ cup oil
- 2 packages (8 ounces each) PHILADELPHIA® Cream Cheese, softened
- 1 container (8 ounces) BREAKSTONE'S® *or* KNUDSEN® Sour Cream
- ½ cup granulated sugar
- 1 teaspoon grated lemon peel
- 1 tablespoon lemon juice
- Powdered sugar

MIX cake mix, 1 egg and oil. Press mixture onto bottom and up sides of greased 15×10×1-inch baking pan. Bake at 350°F for 10 minutes.

BEAT cream cheese with electric mixer on medium speed until smooth. Add remaining 2 eggs, sour cream, granulated sugar, peel and juice; mix until blended. Pour batter into crust.

BAKE at 350°F for 30 to 35 minutes or until filling is just set in center and edges are light golden brown. Cool. Sprinkle with powdered sugar. Cut into bars. Store leftovers in refrigerator.

Makes 2 dozen bars

Streusel Coffeecake

32 CHIPS AHOY!® Chocolate Chip Cookies, divided
1 (18- to 18.5-ounce) package yellow or white cake mix
½ cup sour cream
½ cup PLANTERS® Pecans, chopped
½ cup flaked coconut
¼ cup packed brown sugar
1 teaspoon ground cinnamon
⅓ cup butter, melted
Powdered sugar glaze, optional

1. Coarsely chop 20 cookies; finely crush remaining 12 cookies. Set aside.

2. Prepare cake mix batter according to package directions; stir in sour cream and chopped cookies. Pour into greased and floured 13×9×2-inch baking pan.

3. Mix cookie crumbs, pecans, coconut, brown sugar and cinnamon. Stir in butter; sprinkle over cake batter.

4. Bake at 350°F for 40 minutes or until toothpick inserted in center of cake comes out clean. Cool completely. Drizzle with glaze, if desired. *Makes 24 servings*

Swiss Chocolate Crispies

1 package DUNCAN HINES® Moist Deluxe® Swiss Chocolate Cake Mix
½ cup shortening plus additional for greasing
½ cup butter or margarine, softened
2 eggs
2 tablespoons water
3 cups crispy rice cereal, divided

1. Combine cake mix, ½ cup shortening, butter, eggs and water in large bowl. Beat at low speed with electric mixer for 2 minutes. Fold in 1 cup cereal. Refrigerate 1 hour.

2. Crush remaining 2 cups cereal into coarse crumbs.

3. Preheat oven to 350°F. Grease cookie sheets. Shape dough into 1-inch balls. Roll in crushed cereal. Place on cookie sheets about 1 inch apart.

4. Bake 11 to 13 minutes. Cool 1 minute on cookie sheets. Remove to wire racks.

Makes 4 dozen cookies

Streusel Coffeecake

Brownie Cake Delight

1 package fudge brownie mix
⅓ cup strawberry all-fruit spread
2 cups thawed nondairy whipped topping
¼ teaspoon almond extract
2 cups strawberries, stems removed, halved
¼ cup chocolate sauce

1. Prepare brownies according to package directions, substituting 11×7-inch baking pan. Cool completely in pan.

2. Whisk fruit spread in small bowl until smooth.

3. Combine whipped topping and almond extract in bowl.

4. Cut brownie horizontally in half. Place half of brownie on serving dish. Spread with fruit spread and 1 cup whipped topping. Place second half of brownie, cut side down, over bottom layer. Spread with remaining whipped topping. Place strawberries on whipped topping. Drizzle chocolate sauce over cake before serving. Garnish as desired. *Makes 16 servings*

Snickerdoodles

3 tablespoons sugar
1 teaspoon ground cinnamon
1 package DUNCAN HINES® Moist Deluxe® Yellow Cake Mix
2 eggs
¼ cup vegetable oil

1. Preheat oven to 375°F. Grease cookie sheets. Place sheets of foil on countertop for cooling cookies.

2. Combine sugar and cinnamon in small bowl.

3. Combine cake mix, eggs and oil in large bowl. Stir until well blended. Shape dough into 1-inch balls. Roll in cinnamon-sugar mixture. Place balls 2 inches apart on cookie sheets. Flatten balls with bottom of glass.

4. Bake at 375°F for 8 to 9 minutes or until set. Cool one minute on cookie sheets. Remove to foil to cool completely.
Makes 3 dozen cookies

Brownie Cake Delight

Golden Gingersnaps

- **1 package DUNCAN HINES® Golden Sugar Cookie Mix**
- **1 egg**
- **1 tablespoon water**
- **1 tablespoon light molasses**
- **1½ teaspoons ground ginger**
- **1 teaspoon ground cinnamon**
- **½ teaspoon baking soda**
- **¼ cup granulated sugar**
- **1 tablespoon milk**
- **⅓ cup finely chopped pecans**

1. Preheat oven to 375°F. Grease cookie sheets.

2. Combine cookie mix, egg, water, molasses, ginger, cinnamon and baking soda in large bowl. Stir until thoroughly blended. Drop by level tablespoonfuls into sugar. Roll to completely cover. Place 2 inches apart on prepared cookie sheets. Flatten slightly with bottom of drinking glass. Brush tops lightly with milk. Sprinkle with pecans. Bake 9 minutes for chewy cookies or 10 minutes for crisp cookies. Cool 2 minutes on cookie sheets. Remove to cooling racks. Cool completely. Store in airtight container.

Makes 3 dozen cookies

Pumpkin Snack Bars

Cake

- **1 package (2-layer size) spice cake mix**
- **1 can (16 ounces) pumpkin**
- **¾ cup MIRACLE WHIP® *or* MIRACLE WHIP® LIGHT Dressing**
- **3 eggs**

Frosting

- **3½ cups powdered sugar**
- **½ cup (1 stick) butter, softened**
- **2 tablespoons milk**
- **1 teaspoon vanilla**

Cake

• **BLEND** cake mix, pumpkin, dressing and eggs with electric mixer on medium speed until well blended. Pour into greased 15×10×1-inch baking pan.

• **BAKE** at 350°F 18 to 20 minutes or until toothpick inserted in center comes out clean. Cool completely on wire rack.

Frosting

• **BLEND** all ingredients with electric mixer on low speed until moistened. Beat on high speed until light and fluffy. Spread over cake.

Makes 3 dozen bars

Golden Gingersnaps

Black Forest Cake

MAZOLA NO STICK® Cooking Spray
1 package (18.25 ounces) chocolate cake mix plus ingredients as label directs
Fluffy Frosting (recipe follows)
1 can (21 ounces) cherry pie filling
1 tablespoon cherry flavor liqueur (optional)
2 egg whites

1. Preheat oven to 350°F. Spray 2 (9-inch) round cake pans with cooking spray.

2. Prepare and bake cake mix according to package directions for 2 (9-inch) round layers. Cool on wire rack 10 minutes. Remove from pans; cool completely.

3. Prepare Fluffy Frosting. Place one layer right side up on cake plate. Spoon 1-inch-thick ring of Fluffy Frosting around cake edge.

4. Combine cherry pie filling and liqueur; spoon half onto cake layer, inside frosting ring.

5. Top with second cake layer, bottom side up. Spread a thin layer of frosting over top of cake.

6. Spread a 2-inch-wide ring of frosting around top edge of cake; generously frost side of cake with remaining frosting. Spoon remaining cherry filling on top of cake, inside frosting.

Makes 12 servings

Fluffy Frosting

2 egg whites
1/8 teaspoon salt
1 cup KARO® Light Corn Syrup
1/4 cup sugar
1 1/2 teaspoons vanilla

1. In large bowl with mixer at high speed, beat egg whites and salt until soft peaks form.

2. In small saucepan combine corn syrup and sugar. Stirring constantly, cook over medium-low heat until sugar dissolves and mixture comes to full boil. Remove from heat.

3. Beating constantly, pour hot syrup into egg whites in a fine steady stream. Beat in vanilla. Continue beating until mixture holds stiff peaks. Use immediately. Makes enough to frost a two-layer 8- or 9-inch cake.

Makes about 2 cups

Black Forest Cake

Crispy Thumbprint Cookies

1 package (18.25 ounces) yellow cake mix
½ cup vegetable oil
¼ cup water
1 egg
3 cups crisp rice cereal, crushed
½ cup chopped walnuts
6 tablespoons raspberry preserves

1. Preheat oven to 375°F.

2. Combine cake mix, oil, water and egg. Beat at medium speed of electric mixer until well blended. Add cereal and walnuts; mix until well blended.

3. Drop by heaping teaspoonfuls 2 inches apart onto ungreased baking sheets. Use thumb to make indentation in each cookie. Spoon about ½ teaspoon preserves into center of each cookie.

4. Bake 9 to 11 minutes or until golden brown. Cool cookies 1 minute on baking sheet; remove from baking sheet to wire rack to cool completely.

Makes 3 dozen cookies

Gelatin Poke Cake

1 package (2-layer size) white cake mix or cake mix with pudding in the mix
1 cup boiling water
1 package (4-serving size) JELL-O® Brand Gelatin Dessert, any flavor
½ cup cold water
1 tub (8 ounces) COOL WHIP® Whipped Topping, thawed

HEAT oven to 350°F.

PREPARE and bake cake mix as directed on package for 13×9-inch baking pan. Remove from oven. Cool cake in pan 15 minutes. Pierce cake with large fork at ½-inch intervals.

MEANWHILE, stir boiling water into gelatin in medium bowl at least 2 minutes until completely dissolved. Stir in cold water; carefully pour over cake. Refrigerate 3 hours.

FROST with whipped topping. Refrigerate at least 1 hour or until ready to serve. Decorate as desired. *Makes 15 servings*

Crispy Thumbprint Cookies

Dump Cake

- 1 (20-ounce) can crushed pineapple with juice, undrained
- 1 (21-ounce) can cherry pie filling
- 1 package DUNCAN HINES® Moist Deluxe® Yellow Cake Mix
- 1 cup chopped pecans or walnuts
- ½ cup (1 stick) butter or margarine, cut into thin slices

1. Preheat oven to 350°F. Grease 13×9-inch pan.

2. Dump pineapple with juice into pan. Spread evenly. Dump in pie filling. Spread evenly. Sprinkle cake mix evenly over cherry layer. Sprinkle pecans over cake mix. Dot with butter. Bake 50 minutes or until top is lightly browned. Serve warm or at room temperature.

Makes 12 to 16 servings

Tip: You can use DUNCAN HINES® Moist Deluxe® Pineapple Supreme Cake Mix in place of Moist Deluxe® Yellow Cake Mix.

Quick Peanut Butter Chocolate Chip Cookies

- 1 package DUNCAN HINES® Moist Deluxe® Classic Yellow Cake Mix
- ½ cup creamy peanut butter
- ½ cup butter or margarine, softened
- 2 eggs
- 1 cup milk chocolate chips

1. Preheat oven to 350°F. Grease cookie sheets.

2. Combine cake mix, peanut butter, butter and eggs in large bowl. Mix at low speed with electric mixer until blended. Stir in chocolate chips.

3. Drop by rounded teaspoonfuls onto prepared cookie sheets. Bake 9 to 11 minutes or until lightly browned. Cool 2 minutes on cookie sheets. Remove to cooling racks.

Makes 4 dozen cookies

Tip: Crunchy peanut butter may be substituted for regular peanut butter.

Dump Cake

Abracadabra Cakes

Celebration Pumpkin Cake

1 package (18 ounces) spice cake mix
1 can (16 ounces) pumpkin
3 eggs
¼ cup butter, softened
1½ tubs (16 ounces each) cream cheese frosting
⅓ cup caramel ice cream topping
Pecan halves for garnish

Preheat oven to 350°F. Grease and flour 3 (9-inch) round cake pans. Combine cake mix, pumpkin, eggs and butter in bowl; beat 2 minutes. Divide batter among prepared pans. Bake 20 to 25 minutes or until toothpick inserted in centers comes out clean. Cool 5 minutes on wire rack. Remove from pans; cool completely. Place one cake layer on serving plate; top with frosting. Repeat layers, ending with frosting. Frost cake side. Spread caramel over cake top. Garnish with pecans. *Makes 16 servings*

Celebration Pumpkin Cake

Fudgy Ripple Cake

1 package (18.25 ounces) yellow cake mix plus ingredients to prepare mix
1 package (3 ounces) cream cheese, softened
2 tablespoons unsweetened cocoa powder
Fudgy Glaze (recipe follows)
½ cup "M&M's"® Chocolate Mini Baking Bits

Preheat oven to 350°F. Grease and flour 10-inch bundt pan; set aside. Prepare cake batter as package directs. In bowl mix 1½ cups batter, cream cheese and cocoa powder until smooth. Pour half of yellow batter into prepared pan. Drop spoonfuls of chocolate batter over yellow batter in pan. Top with remaining yellow batter. Bake about 45 minutes or until toothpick inserted in center comes out clean. Cool on wire rack. Invert cake onto serving plate. Prepare Fudgy Glaze; spread over cake, allowing some to run over side. Sprinkle with "M&M's"® Chocolate Mini Baking Bits.

Makes 10 servings

Fudgy Glaze

1 square (1 ounce) semi-sweet chocolate
1 cup powdered sugar
⅓ cup unsweetened cocoa powder
3 tablespoons milk
½ teaspoon vanilla extract

Place chocolate in small microwave-safe bowl. Microwave at HIGH 30 seconds; stir. Repeat as necessary until chocolate is melted, stirring at 10-second intervals; set aside. In medium bowl combine powdered sugar and cocoa powder. Stir in milk, vanilla and chocolate until smooth.

Magical Tip

To soften cream cheese quickly, remove it from the wrapper and place it on a microwave-safe plate. Microwave at MEDIUM (50% power) 15 to 20 seconds or until softened.

Fudgy Ripple Cake

Fantasy Angel Food Cake

1 package DUNCAN HINES® Angel Food Cake Mix
Red and green food coloring
1 container DUNCAN HINES® Cream Cheese Frosting

1. Preheat oven to 350°F.

2. Prepare cake following package directions. Divide batter into thirds and place in 3 different bowls. Add a few drops red food coloring to one. Add a few drops green food coloring to another. Stir each until blended. Leave third one plain. Spoon pink batter into ungreased 10-inch tube pan. Cover with white batter and top with green batter. Bake and cool following package directions.

3. To make glaze, heat frosting in microwave at HIGH (100% power) 20 to 30 seconds. Do not overheat. Stir until smooth. Set aside 1/4 cup warm glaze. Spoon remaining glaze on top and side of cake to cover. Divide remaining glaze in half and place in 2 bowls. Add a few drops red food coloring to one. Add a few drops green food coloring to the other. Stir each until blended. Drizzle green glaze around cake edge so it runs down side. Repeat with pink glaze.

Makes 16 servings

Cran-Lemon Coffee Cake

1 package (18.25 ounces) yellow cake mix with pudding in the mix
1 cup water
1/3 cup butter, melted
1/4 cup fresh lemon juice
3 eggs
1 tablespoon grated lemon peel
1 1/2 cups chopped cranberries

- Preheat oven to 350°F. Grease and flour 12-inch tube pan. Beat cake mix, water, butter, lemon juice, eggs and lemon peel in bowl until well blended. Fold in cranberries. Spread batter in pan.
- Bake about 55 minutes or until toothpick inserted in center comes out clean. Cool on wire rack about 10 minutes. Remove from pan; let cool. *Makes 12 servings*

Fantasy Angel Food Cake

Pecan Spice Cake

MAZOLA NO STICK® Cooking Spray
1 package (18.25 ounces) spice cake mix plus ingredients as label directs
½ cup finely chopped pecans
Coconut-Pecan Filling (recipe follows)
Luscious Chocolate Frosting (recipe follows)

1. Preheat oven to 350°F. Spray 2 (9-inch) round cake pans with cooking spray. Prepare cake mix as label directs; stir in pecans. Pour batter into pans.

2. Bake as directed. Cool on wire racks 10 minutes. Remove from pans; cool completely. When cool, split layers horizontally in half.

3. Place one cake layer on serving plate. Spread with ⅓ of Coconut-Pecan Filling. Top with second cake layer; spread with about ⅔ cup Luscious Chocolate Frosting. Top with third cake layer; spread with ⅓ of filling. Top with fourth cake layer. Frost side of cake with remaining frosting; spread top of cake with remaining filling. Refrigerate 2 hours or until set.

Makes 12 to 16 servings

Coconut-Pecan Filling

½ cup KARO® Light Corn Syrup
¾ cup sugar
½ cup evaporated milk
½ cup (1 stick) butter
3 egg yolks, slightly beaten
1 teaspoon vanilla
1⅓ cups flaked coconut
1 cup finely chopped pecans

In saucepan mix corn syrup, sugar, milk, butter, egg yolks and vanilla. Cook and stir over medium heat until thickened, 10 to 12 minutes. Remove from heat. Stir in coconut and pecans. Cool until thick and spreadable. *Makes 2¼ cups*

Luscious Chocolate Frosting

1 package (3 ounces) cream cheese
¼ cup KARO® Light Corn Syrup
2 tablespoons butter
2 cups confectioners' sugar
⅓ cup unsweetened cocoa
½ teaspoon vanilla

In bowl beat cream cheese, corn syrup and butter until creamy. Beat in confectioners' sugar, cocoa and vanilla until frosting is of spreading consistency. *Makes 1⅓ cups*

Pecan Spice Cake

Coconut Jam Cake

1 package (2-layer size) yellow cake mix
1 package (7 ounces) BAKER'S® ANGEL FLAKE Coconut, divided
½ cup strawberry jam
1 tub (8 ounces) COOL WHIP® Whipped Topping, thawed
½ cup apricot jam
Sliced fresh strawberries
Canned apricot halves, drained
Fresh mint leaves

HEAT oven to 350°F.

PREPARE and bake cake mix as directed on package for 2 (9-inch) round cake layers, gently stirring 1 cup coconut into batter just before pouring into pans. Cool 10 minutes; remove from pans. Cool completely on wire racks.

PLACE 1 cake layer on serving plate; spread with strawberry jam. Spread ¾ cup whipped topping over jam; top with second cake layer. Spread top of cake with apricot jam. Frost top and side of cake with remaining whipped topping. Pat remaining coconut onto side of cake.

REFRIGERATE until ready to serve. Garnish with fruit and mint just before serving.

Makes 12 servings

Coconut Jam Cake

Chocolate Banana Cake

Cake

1 package DUNCAN HINES® Moist Deluxe® Devil's Food Cake Mix
3 eggs
1⅓ cups milk
½ cup vegetable oil

Topping

1 package (4-serving size) banana cream instant pudding and pie filling mix
1 cup milk
1 cup whipping cream, whipped
1 medium banana
Lemon juice
Chocolate sprinkles

1. Preheat oven to 350°F. Grease and flour 13×9×2-inch pan.

2. For cake, combine cake mix, eggs, milk and oil in large bowl. Beat at low speed with electric mixer until moistened. Beat at medium speed 2 minutes. Pour into pan. Bake at 350°F 35 to 38 minutes or until toothpick inserted in center comes out clean. Cool completely.

3. For topping, combine pudding mix and milk in large bowl. Stir until smooth. Fold in whipped cream. Spread on top of cooled cake. Slice banana; dip in lemon juice, arrange on top. Garnish with chocolate sprinkles. Refrigerate until ready to serve.

Makes 12 to 16 servings

Cherry-Mallow Cake

4 cups miniature marshmallows (about ¾ of 10½-ounce package)
1 (18.25-ounce) package yellow cake mix
1 (21-ounce) can cherry pie filling

Spray 13×9×2-inch baking pan with vegetable spray. Place marshmallows evenly in bottom of pan.

Prepare cake mix according to package directions. Pour batter over marshmallows. Spoon cherry filling evenly over cake batter.

Bake in preheated 350°F oven 30 to 40 minutes. Top of cake will be bubbly and marshmallows will be sticky. Let cool before serving.

Makes 15 servings

Favorite recipe from **Cherry Marketing Institute**

Black and White Pistachio Cake

Cake

1 package (18¼ ounces) marble cake mix
3 eggs
1¼ cups water
⅓ cup vegetable oil
½ teaspoon vanilla

Filling

2 packages (4-serving size each) pistachio instant pudding and pie filling mix
3 cups milk
⅓ cup chopped maraschino cherries, drained
¼ cup chopped pistachio nuts

Frosting

1¼ cups cold milk
1 package (4-serving size) pistachio instant pudding and pie filling mix
2 envelopes whipped topping mix
Additional maraschino cherries and pistachio nuts (optional)

Cake

Preheat oven to 350°F. Lightly grease and flour two 8-inch round cake pans.

Combine cake mix, eggs, water, oil and vanilla in large bowl. Mix according to package directions. Pour half of batter into one pan. Stir contents of chocolate packet into remaining batter. Pour chocolate batter into second pan. Bake and cool according to package directions.

Filling

Prepare pudding mix using 3 cups milk. Stir in chopped cherries and pistachios. Cover and refrigerate until ready to use.

Frosting

Combine milk, pudding mix and whipped topping mix in large bowl. Beat at low speed with electric mixer until blended. Beat at high speed 2 to 3 minutes or until stiff, scraping side of bowl often.

To assemble cake, split each cake layer in half. Alternate chocolate cake layer with white cake layer, spreading filling between each layer. Frost top and side of cake with frosting. Garnish with additional maraschino cherries and pistachios, if desired.

Makes 12 to 16 servings

Black and White Pistachio Cake

Triple Chocolate Fantasy

Cake

1 package DUNCAN HINES® Moist Deluxe® Devil's Food Cake Mix
3 eggs
1⅓ cups water
½ cup vegetable oil
½ cup ground walnuts

Chocolate Glaze

1 package (12 ounces) semisweet chocolate chips
¼ cup plus 2 tablespoons butter or margarine
¼ cup chopped walnuts

White Chocolate Glaze

3 ounces white chocolate, coarsely chopped
1 tablespoon shortening

1. Preheat oven to 350°F. Grease and flour 10-inch Bundt® pan.

2. For cake, combine cake mix, eggs, water, oil and ground walnuts in large bowl. Beat for 2 minutes. Pour into pan.

3. Bake at 350°F 45 to 55 minutes or until toothpick inserted in center comes out clean. Cool in pan 25 minutes. Invert onto serving plate. Cool completely.

4. For chocolate glaze, combine chocolate chips and butter in small heavy saucepan. Heat on low heat until chips are melted. Stir constantly until shiny and smooth. (Glaze will be very thick.) Spread hot glaze over cooled cake. Sprinkle with chopped walnuts.

5. For white chocolate glaze, mix white chocolate and shortening in small heavy saucepan. Heat on low heat until melted, stirring constantly. Drizzle hot glaze over top and side of cake.

Makes 12 to 16 servings

Magical Tip

To reduce the risk of overprocessing when grinding nuts in a food processor, add a small amount of the flour or cake mix from the recipe. If they are overprocessed, nuts will become nut butter.

Triple Chocolate Fantasy

Magical Kids' Treats

Chocolate Peanut Butter Cups

1 package DUNCAN HINES® Moist Deluxe® Swiss Chocolate Cake Mix
1 container DUNCAN HINES® Vanilla Frosting
½ cup creamy peanut butter
15 miniature peanut butter cup candies, wrappers removed, cut in half vertically

1. Preheat oven to 350°F. Place 30 (2½-inch) paper liners in muffin cups.

2. Prepare, bake and cool cupcakes following package directions for basic recipe.

3. Combine Vanilla frosting and peanut butter in medium bowl. Stir until smooth. Frost one cupcake. Decorate with peanut butter cup candy, cut-side down. Repeat with remaining cupcakes and candies.

Makes 30 servings

Chocolate Peanut Butter Cups

Gummy Purple Dinosaur Cake

1 tub (8 ounces) COOL WHIP® Whipped Topping, thawed
Few drops blue and red food coloring
1 baked 13×9-inch cake, any flavor except angel food, cooled
Gumdrops
Assorted small candies

TINT whipped topping purple with blue and red food colorings in small bowl with wire whisk.

CUT cake as shown in Diagram 1.

USING small amount of whipped topping to hold pieces together, arrange cake on serving tray as shown in Diagram 2. Frost cake with remaining whipped topping. Decorate with gumdrops and candies. Serve immediately. Store leftover cake in refrigerator.

Makes 12 to 16 servings

1

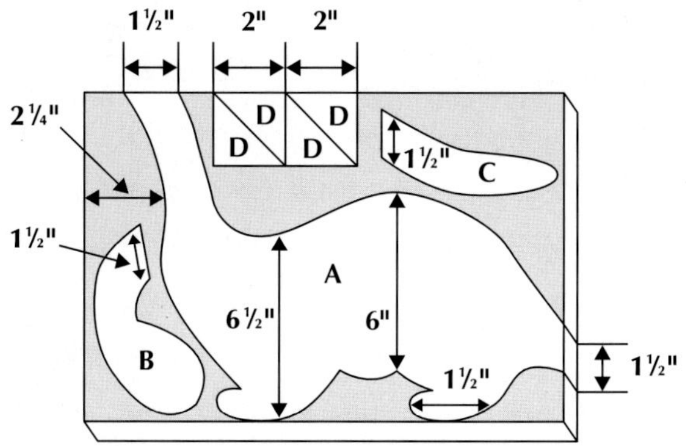

2

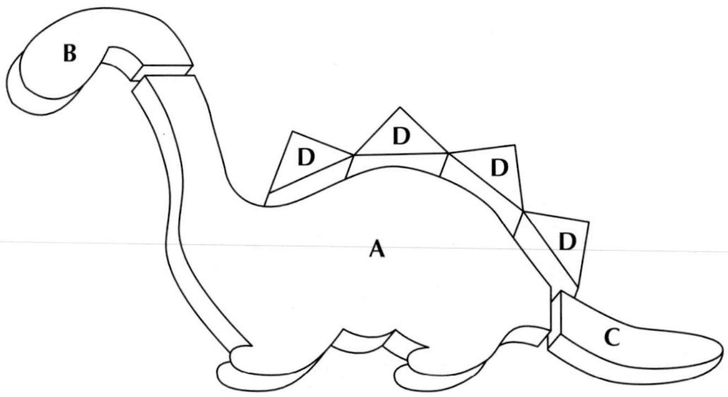

Gummy Purple Dinosaur Cake

Rich Chocolate Caramel Brownies

1 package (18.25 to 18.5 ounces) devil's food or chocolate cake mix
1 cup chopped nuts
½ cup (1 stick) butter or margarine, melted
1 cup undiluted CARNATION® Evaporated Milk, divided
35 (10 ounces) light caramels, unwrapped
1 cup (6 ounces) NESTLÉ® TOLL HOUSE® Semi-Sweet Chocolate Morsels

COMBINE cake mix and nuts in large bowl; stir in butter. Stir in *⅔ cup* evaporated milk (batter will be thick). Spread *half* of batter into greased 13×9-inch baking pan. Bake in preheated 350°F. oven for 15 minutes.

COMBINE caramels and *remaining* evaporated milk in small saucepan. Cook over low heat, stirring constantly, for about 10 minutes or until caramels are melted. Sprinkle chocolate morsels over baked layer; drizzle caramel mixture over top. Drop *remaining* batter by heaping teaspoon over caramel mixture. Bake for additional 20 to 25 minutes (top layer will be soft). Cool completely on wire rack.

Makes about 48 brownies

Variation: For Rich Chocolate Butterscotch Brownies, pour 12.25-ounce jar of butterscotch-flavored topping over Nestlé® Toll House® Semi-Sweet Chocolate Morsels, instead of melting caramels with ⅓ cup evaporated milk.

Magical Tip

For easy removal of brownies and bar cookies (and no cleanup!), line the baking pan with foil and leave at least 3 inches hanging over each end. Use the foil to lift out the treats, place them on a cutting board and carefully remove the foil. Then simply cut them into pieces.

Double Nut Chocolate Chip Cookies

1 package DUNCAN HINES® Moist Deluxe® Yellow Cake Mix
½ cup butter or margarine, melted
1 egg
1 cup semisweet chocolate chips
½ cup finely chopped pecans
1 cup sliced almonds, divided

1. Preheat oven to 375°F. Grease cookie sheets.

2. Combine cake mix, butter and egg in large bowl. Mix at low speed with electric mixer until just blended. Stir in chocolate chips, pecans and ¼ cup almonds. Shape rounded tablespoonfuls of dough into balls. Place remaining ¾ cup almonds in shallow bowl. Press tops of cookies in almonds. Place 1 inch apart on prepared cookie sheets.

3. Bake 9 to 11 minutes or until lightly browned. Cool 2 minutes on cookie sheets. Remove to cooling racks.

Makes 3 to 3½ dozen cookies

Double Nut Chocolate Chip Cookies

I Think You're "Marbleous" Cupcakes

1 box (18½ ounces) pudding-in-the-mix cake mix, any flavor
1¼ cups water
3 eggs
¼ cup oil
1 tub (16 ounces) vanilla frosting
1 tube (4¼ ounces) red decorating icing

Supplies

Decorating tips to fit tube of icing

1. Preheat oven to 350°F. Grease or paper-line 24 (2½-inch) muffin cups. Prepare cake mix according to package directions with water, eggs and oil. Spoon batter into prepared cups, filling each ⅔ full.

2. Bake 20 to 25 minutes or until toothpick inserted into centers comes out clean. Cool in pans 20 minutes. Remove to wire rack; cool completely.

3. Spread 1½ to 2 tablespoons frosting over each cupcake. Fit round tip onto tube of icing. Squeeze 4 to 5 dots icing over each cupcake. Swirl toothpick through icing and frosting to marbleize or make heart shapes.

Makes 2 dozen cupcakes

Oreo® Pizza

14 Regular or Reduced Fat OREO® Chocolate Sandwich Cookies, chopped (about 1½ cups)
1 (21-ounce) package brownie mix, batter prepared according to package directions
1 cup JET-PUFFED® Miniature Marshmallows
⅓ cup PLANTERS® Walnuts, chopped
⅓ cup candy-coated peanut butter candies

1. Stir cookie pieces into prepared brownie batter; spread in greased 14-inch pizza pan. Bake at 350°F for 18 to 20 minutes or until done.

2. Sprinkle marshmallows over hot brownie; bake 2 to 3 minutes or until marshmallows are puffed.

3. Sprinkle with nuts and candies; pressing lightly into softened marshmallows. Cool.

Makes 8 servings

I Think You're "Marbleous" Cupcakes

Banana Split Cake

1 package DUNCAN HINES® Moist Deluxe® Banana Supreme Cake Mix
3 eggs
1⅓ cups water
½ cup all-purpose flour
⅓ cup vegetable oil
1 cup semi-sweet mini chocolate chips
2 to 3 bananas
1 can (16 ounces) chocolate syrup
1 container (8 ounces) frozen whipped topping, thawed
½ cup chopped walnuts
Colored sprinkles
Maraschino cherries with stems, for garnish

1. Preheat oven to 350°F. Grease and flour 13×9×2-inch pan.

2. Combine cake mix, eggs, water, flour and oil in large bowl. Beat at low speed with electric mixer until moistened. Beat at medium speed 2 minutes. Stir in chocolate chips. Pour into pan. Bake at 350°F 32 to 35 minutes or until toothpick inserted in center comes out clean. Cool completely.

3. Slice bananas. Cut cake into squares; top with banana slices. Drizzle with chocolate syrup. Top with whipped topping, walnuts and sprinkles. Garnish with maraschino cherries.

Makes 12 to 16 servings

Tip: Dip bananas in diluted lemon juice to prevent darkening.

Chewy Chocolate Cookies

1 package (2-layer size) chocolate cake mix
2 eggs
1 cup MIRACLE WHIP® *or* MIRACLE WHIP® LIGHT Dressing
1 cup BAKER'S® Semi-Sweet Real Chocolate Chips
½ cup chopped walnuts

- **MIX** cake mix, eggs and dressing in large bowl with electric mixer on medium speed until blended. Stir in remaining ingredients.
- **DROP** by rounded teaspoonfuls onto greased cookie sheets.
- **BAKE** at 350°F 10 to 12 minutes or until edges are lightly browned.

Makes 4 dozen cookies

Banana Split Cake

Boston Babies

1 package (18¼ ounces) yellow cake mix
3 eggs *or* ¾ cup cholesterol-free egg substitute
⅓ cup unsweetened applesauce
1 package (4-serving size) sugar-free vanilla pudding and pie filling mix
2 cups low-fat (1%) milk or fat-free (skim) milk
⅓ cup sugar
⅓ cup unsweetened cocoa powder
1 tablespoon cornstarch
1½ cups water
1½ teaspoons vanilla

1. Line 24 (2½-inch) muffin cups with paper liners; set aside.

2. Prepare cake mix according to lower fat package directions, using 3 eggs and applesauce. Pour batter into prepared muffin cups. Bake according to package directions; cool completely. Freeze 12 cupcakes for another use.

3. Prepare pudding according to package directions, using 2 cups milk; cover and refrigerate.

4. Combine sugar, cocoa, cornstarch and water in large microwavable bowl; whisk until smooth. Microwave at HIGH 4 to 6 minutes, stirring every 2 minutes, until slightly thickened. Stir in vanilla.

5. To serve, drizzle 2 tablespoons chocolate glaze over each dessert plate. Cut cupcakes in half; place 2 halves on top of chocolate on each dessert plate. Top each with about 2 heaping tablespoonfuls pudding. Garnish if desired. Serve immediately.

Makes 12 servings

Magical Tip

These treats are a great low-fat snack! Each serving has 158 calories and only 4 grams of fat.

Boston Baby

Oatmeal Brownie Gems

2¾ cups quick-cooking oats, uncooked
1 cup all-purpose flour
1 cup packed brown sugar
1 cup chopped walnuts
1 teaspoon baking soda
1 cup butter, melted
1¾ cups "M&M's"® Semi-Sweet Chocolate Mini Baking Bits
1 (19- to 21-ounce) package fudge brownie mix, prepared according to package directions for fudge-like brownies

Preheat oven to 350°F. In large bowl combine oats, flour, sugar, nuts and baking soda; add butter until mixture forms coarse crumbs. Toss in "M&M's"® Semi-Sweet Chocolate Mini Baking Bits until evenly distributed. Reserve 3 cups mixture. Pat remaining mixture onto bottom of 15×10×1-inch pan to form crust. Pour prepared brownie mix over crust, spreading into thin layer. Sprinkle reserved crumb mixture over top of brownie mixture; pat down lightly. Bake 25 to 30 minutes or until toothpick inserted in center comes out with moist crumbs. Cool completely. Cut into bars. *Makes 48 bars*

Chocolate Sundae Cupcakes

24 REYNOLDS® Bake Cups
1 package (about 18 ounces) devil's food cake mix
1 container (16 ounces) chocolate frosting
½ cup caramel ice cream topping
1½ cups frozen whipped topping, thawed
24 maraschino cherries with stems, drained

PREHEAT oven to 350°F. Place Reynolds Bake Cups in muffin pans; set aside. Prepare cake mix following package directions for 24 cupcakes. Spoon batter into bake cups. Bake as directed. Cool.

FROST cupcakes. Top each cupcake with 1 teaspoon caramel topping and 1 tablespoon whipped topping. Garnish each cupcake with a cherry. Refrigerate until serving time.

Makes 24 cupcakes

Oatmeal Brownie Gems

Recipe for Oatmeal Brownie Gems
From Josephine
Serves
Ingredients:
2 3/4 cups quick-cooking or old
fashioned oats, uncooked
1 cup all-purpose flour
1 cup firmly packed brown sugar
1 tsp. baking soda.

Kids' Confetti Cake

Cake

- 1 package **DUNCAN HINES® Moist Deluxe® Yellow Cake Mix**
- **1 package (4-serving size) vanilla instant pudding and pie filling mix**
- **4 eggs**
- **1 cup water**
- **½ cup vegetable oil**
- **1 cup semi-sweet mini chocolate chips**

Topping

- **1 cup colored miniature marshmallows**
- **⅔ cup DUNCAN HINES® Chocolate Frosting**
- **2 tablespoons semi-sweet mini chocolate chips**

1. Preheat oven to 350°F. Lightly grease and flour 13×9×2-inch baking pan.

2. For cake, combine cake mix, pudding mix, eggs, water and oil in large bowl. Beat at medium speed with electric mixer 2 minutes. Stir in 1 cup chocolate chips. Pour into pan. Bake 40 to 45 minutes or until toothpick inserted in center comes out clean.

3. For topping, immediately arrange marshmallows evenly over hot cake. Place frosting in microwave-safe bowl. Microwave at HIGH (100% power) 25 to 30 seconds. Stir until smooth. Drizzle over marshmallows and cake. Sprinkle with 2 tablespoons chocolate chips. Cool completely.

Makes 12 to 16 servings

Magical Tip

To grease and flour cake pans, use a paper towel, waxed paper or your fingers to apply a thin, even layer of shortening. Sprinkle flour into the greased pan; shake or tilt the pan to coat evenly with flour, then tap lightly to remove any excess.

Kids' Confetti Cake

Double Dip Ice Cream Cone Cakes

- **1 package (2-layer size) cake mix, any flavor**
- **4 squares BAKER'S® Semi-Sweet Chocolate**
- **¼ cup milk**
- **1 tub (8 ounces) COOL WHIP® Whipped Topping, thawed**
- **Assorted small candies**
- **Multicolored sprinkles**
- **Maraschino cherries**

HEAT oven to 350°F.

PREPARE cake mix as directed on package. Divide batter evenly between greased and floured 8-inch round and 8-inch square baking pans. Bake as directed on package. Cool 10 minutes; remove from pans. Cool completely on wire racks.

CUT cakes as shown in Diagrams 1 and 2. Assemble pieces on large serving trays as shown in Diagrams 3 and 4.

MICROWAVE chocolate and milk in medium microwavable bowl on HIGH 2 minutes or until chocolate is almost melted. Stir until chocolate is completely melted. Cool 20 minutes or until room temperature. Gently stir 1½ cups whipped topping into chocolate with wire whisk until blended.

FROST "cones" with chocolate whipped topping mixture; decorate with candies, if desired. Frost "ice cream" with remaining whipped topping; decorate with sprinkles.

REFRIGERATE until ready to serve. Top with cherries just before serving.

Makes 12 to 14 servings

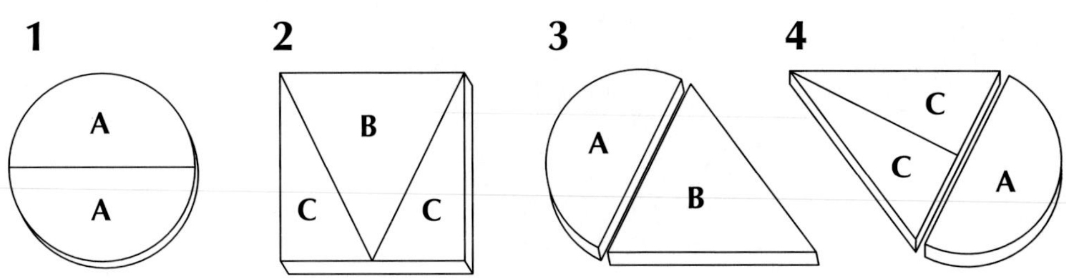

Double Dip Ice Cream Cone Cake

Quick-as-a-Wink Cookies

Chocolate Chip 'n Oatmeal Cookies

1 package (18.25 or 18.5 ounces) yellow cake mix
1 cup quick-cooking rolled oats, uncooked
¾ cup butter or margarine, softened
2 eggs
1 cup HERSHEY®S Semi-Sweet Chocolate Chips

1. Heat oven to 350°F.

2. Combine cake mix, oats, butter and eggs in large bowl; mix well. Stir in chocolate chips. Drop by rounded teaspoons onto ungreased cookie sheets.

3. Bake 10 to 12 minutes or until very lightly browned. Cool slightly; remove from cookie sheets to wire racks. Cool completely.

Makes 4 dozen cookies

Chocolate Chip 'n Oatmeal Cookies

Pinwheel Cookies

½ cup shortening plus additional for greasing
⅓ cup plus 1 tablespoon butter, softened and divided
2 egg yolks
½ teaspoon vanilla
1 package DUNCAN HINES® Moist Deluxe® Fudge Marble Cake Mix

1. Combine ½ cup shortening, ⅓ cup butter, egg yolks and vanilla in large bowl. Mix at low speed of electric mixer until blended. Set aside cocoa packet from cake mix. Gradually add cake mix. Blend well.

2. Divide dough in half. Add cocoa packet and remaining 1 tablespoon butter to one half of dough. Knead until well blended and chocolate colored.

3. Roll out yellow dough between two pieces of waxed paper into 18×12×⅛-inch rectangle. Repeat for chocolate dough. Remove top pieces of waxed paper from chocolate and yellow doughs. Place yellow dough directly on top of chocolate dough. Remove remaining layers of waxed paper. Roll up jelly-roll fashion, beginning at wide side. Refrigerate 2 hours.

4. Preheat oven to 350°F. Grease cookie sheets.

5. Cut dough into ⅛-inch slices. Place sliced dough 1 inch apart on prepared cookie sheets. Bake 9 to 11 minutes or until lightly browned. Cool 5 minutes on cookie sheets. Remove to cooling racks.

Makes 3½ dozen cookies

Magical Tip

Use gentle pressure and a back-and-forth sawing motion when slicing the roll of cookie dough, so the cookies will keep their nice round shape. Rotating the roll while slicing also prevents one side from flattening.

Pinwheel Cookies

Cheesecake-Topped Brownies

1 (21- or 23.6-ounce) package fudge brownie mix
1 (8-ounce) package cream cheese, softened
2 tablespoons butter, softened
1 tablespoon cornstarch
1 (14-ounce) can EAGLE® BRAND Sweetened Condensed Milk (NOT evaporated milk)
1 egg
2 teaspoons vanilla extract
Ready-to-spread chocolate frosting (optional)
Orange peel (optional)

1. Preheat oven to 350°F. Prepare brownie mix as package directs. Spread in well-greased 13×9-inch baking pan.

2. Beat cream cheese, butter and cornstarch until fluffy. Beat in Eagle Brand, egg and vanilla until smooth. Pour cheesecake mixture over brownie batter.

3. Bake 40 to 45 minutes or until top is lightly browned. Cool. Spread with frosting or sprinkle with orange peel, if desired. Store covered in refrigerator.

Makes 36 to 40 brownies

Banana Chocolate Chip Cookies

2 extra-ripe, medium DOLE® Bananas, peeled
1 package (17.5 ounces) chocolate chip cookie mix
½ teaspoon ground cinnamon
1 egg, lightly beaten
1 teaspoon vanilla extract
1 cup toasted wheat germ

• Mash bananas with fork. Measure 1 cup.

• Combine cookie mix and cinnamon. Stir in contents of enclosed flavoring packet, mashed bananas, egg and vanilla until well blended. Stir in wheat germ.

• Drop batter by heaping tablespoonfuls 2 inches apart onto cookie sheets coated with cooking spray. Shape cookies with back of spoon. Bake in 375°F oven 10 to 12 minutes until lightly browned. Cool on wire racks.

Makes 18 cookies

Cheesecake-Topped Brownies

Coconut Clouds

2⅔ cups flaked coconut, divided
1 package DUNCAN HINES® Moist Deluxe® Yellow Cake Mix
1 egg
½ cup vegetable oil
¼ cup water
1 teaspoon almond extract

1. Preheat oven to 350°F. Place 1⅓ cups coconut in medium bowl; set aside.

2. Combine cake mix, egg, oil, water and almond extract in large bowl. Beat at low speed with electric mixer. Stir in remaining 1⅓ cups reserved coconut. Drop rounded teaspoonful dough into reserved coconut. Roll to cover lightly. Place on ungreased baking sheet. Repeat with remaining dough, placing balls 2 inches apart.

3. Bake at 350°F 10 to 12 minutes or until light golden brown. Let cool 1 minute on baking sheets. Remove to cooling racks. Cool completely. Store in airtight container.

Makes 3½ dozen cookies

Coconut Clouds

Chocolate Caramel Pecan Squares

1 (14-ounce) package caramels, unwrapped
⅔ cup evaporated milk, divided
1 (18.25-ounce) package German chocolate cake mix (pudding style)
½ cup butter, melted
1 (6-ounce) package semi-sweet chocolate chips
1 cup chopped pecans, divided

Preheat oven to 350°F. Melt caramels with ⅓ cup evaporated milk in saucepan over low heat until smooth, stirring often. Combine cake mix, butter and remaining ⅓ cup evaporated milk. Press half of cake mixture into greased 13×9-inch baking pan. Bake 6 minutes. Remove from oven. Sprinkle top with chocolate chips and ½ cup pecans. Top with caramel mixture, spreading to edges of pan. Spoon remaining cake mixture over top and sprinkle with remaining ½ cup pecans. Bake 20 minutes. Cut into squares. Serve warm or cool completely.

Makes 24 squares

Peanut Butter Marbled Brownies

4 ounces cream cheese, softened
½ cup peanut butter
2 tablespoons sugar
1 egg
1 package (20 to 22 ounces) brownie mix plus ingredients to prepare mix
¾ cup lightly salted cocktail peanuts

• Preheat oven to 350°F. Grease 13×9-inch baking pan; set aside.

• Beat cream cheese, peanut butter, sugar and egg in medium bowl until blended.

• Prepare brownie mix according to package directions. Spread brownie batter in prepared pan. Spoon peanut butter mixture in dollops over batter; swirl with tip of knife. Sprinkle peanuts on top; lightly press into batter.

• Bake 30 to 35 minutes or until toothpick inserted into center comes out almost clean. Do not overbake. Cool in pan on wire rack. Cut into 2-inch squares.

Makes 2 dozen brownies

Festive Fudge Blossoms

- **¼ cup butter, softened**
- **1 box (18.25 ounces) chocolate fudge cake mix**
- **1 egg, slightly beaten**
- **2 tablespoons water**
- **¾ to 1 cup finely chopped walnuts**
- **48 chocolate star candies**

1. Preheat oven to 350°F. Cut butter into cake mix in large bowl until mixture resembles coarse crumbs. Stir in egg and water until well blended.

2. Shape dough into ½-inch balls; roll in walnuts, pressing nuts gently into dough. Place about 2 inches apart on ungreased baking sheets.

3. Bake cookies 12 minutes or until puffed and nearly set. Place chocolate star in center of each cookie; bake 1 minute more. Cool 2 minutes on baking sheet. Remove cookies from baking sheets to wire rack to cool completely.

Makes 4 dozen cookies

Prep and Bake Time: 30 minutes

Apricot Crumb Squares

- **1 package (18.25 ounces) light yellow cake mix**
- **1 teaspoon ground cinnamon**
- **½ teaspoon ground nutmeg**
- **6 tablespoons cold butter, cut into pieces**
- **¾ cup uncooked multigrain oatmeal cereal**
- **1 whole egg**
- **2 egg whites**
- **1 tablespoon water**
- **1 jar (10 ounces) apricot fruit spread**
- **2 tablespoons firmly packed light brown sugar**

• Preheat oven to 350°F. Combine cake mix, cinnamon and nutmeg in bowl. Cut in butter with pastry blender until coarse crumbs form. Stir in cereal. Reserve 1 cup mixture. Mix egg, egg whites and water into remaining mixture.

• Spread batter in ungreased 13×9-inch baking pan. Top with fruit spread; sprinkle with reserved mixture. Top with brown sugar.

• Bake 35 to 40 minutes or until golden brown. Cool in pan on wire rack. *Makes 15 squares*

Festive Fudge Blossoms

Cinnamon Stars

2 tablespoons sugar
¾ teaspoon ground cinnamon
¾ cup butter or margarine, softened
2 egg yolks
1 teaspoon vanilla extract
1 package DUNCAN HINES® Moist Deluxe® French Vanilla Cake Mix

1. Preheat oven to 375°F. Combine sugar and cinnamon in small bowl. Set aside.

2. Combine butter, egg yolks and vanilla extract in large bowl. Blend in cake mix gradually. Roll to ⅛-inch thickness on lightly floured surface. Cut with 2½-inch star cookie cutter. Place 2 inches apart on ungreased baking sheet.

3. Sprinkle cookies with cinnamon-sugar mixture. Bake at 375°F for 6 to 8 minutes or until edges are light golden brown. Cool 1 minute on baking sheet. Remove to cooling rack. Cool completely. Store in airtight container.

Makes 3 to 3½ dozen cookies

Fudgy Oatmeal Butterscotch Cookies

1 package (18.25 ounces) devil's food cake mix
1½ cups quick-cooking or old-fashioned oats, uncooked
¾ cup (1½ sticks) butter, melted
2 large eggs
1 tablespoon vegetable oil
1 teaspoon vanilla extract
1¼ cups "M&M's"® Chocolate Mini Baking Bits
1 cup butterscotch chips

Preheat oven to 350°F. In large bowl combine cake mix, oats, butter, eggs, oil and vanilla until well blended. Stir in "M&M's"® Chocolate Mini Baking Bits and butterscotch chips. Drop by heaping tablespoonfuls 2 inches apart onto ungreased cookie sheets. Bake 10 to 12 minutes. Cool 1 minute on cookie sheets; cool completely on wire racks. Store in tightly covered container.

Makes 3 dozen cookies

Cinnamon Stars

Quick Chocolate Softies

- **1 package (18.25 ounces) devil's food cake mix**
- **⅓ cup water**
- **¼ cup butter, softened**
- **1 egg**
- **1 cup white chocolate baking chips**
- **½ cup coarsely chopped walnuts**

• Preheat oven to 350°F. Grease cookie sheets. Combine cake mix, water, butter and egg in large bowl. Beat with electric mixer at low speed until moistened. Increase speed to medium; beat 1 minute. (Dough will be thick.) Stir in white chocolate chips and nuts; mix until well blended. Drop dough by heaping teaspoonfuls 2 inches apart onto prepared cookie sheets.

• Bake 10 to 12 minutes or until set. Let cookies stand on cookie sheets 1 minute. Remove cookies to wire racks; cool completely.

Makes 4 dozen cookies

Maple Walnut Bars

- **1 package DUNCAN HINES® Moist Deluxe® Classic Yellow Cake Mix, divided**
- **⅓ cup butter, melted**
- **4 eggs, divided**
- **1⅓ cups MRS. BUTTERWORTH® Maple Syrup**
- **⅓ cup packed light brown sugar**
- **½ teaspoon vanilla extract**
- **1 cup chopped walnuts**

1. Preheat oven to 350°F. Grease 13×9-inch pan.

2. Reserve ⅔ cup cake mix; set aside. Combine remaining cake mix, melted butter and 1 egg in large bowl. Stir until thoroughly blended. (Mixture will be crumbly.) Press into prepared pan. Bake 15 to 20 minutes or until light golden brown.

3. Combine reserved cake mix, maple syrup, remaining 3 eggs, sugar and vanilla in large bowl. Beat at low speed with electric mixer for 3 minutes. Pour over crust. Sprinkle with walnuts. Bake 30 to 35 minutes or until filling is set. Cool completely in pan. Cut into bars. Store in refrigerator.

Makes 24 bars

Quick Chocolate Softies

Lemon Bars

- 1 package DUNCAN HINES® Moist Deluxe® Lemon Supreme Cake Mix
- 3 eggs, divided
- 1/3 cup butter-flavor shortening
- 1/2 cup granulated sugar
- 1/4 cup lemon juice
- 2 teaspoons grated lemon peel
- 1/2 teaspoon baking powder
- 1/4 teaspoon salt
- Confectioners' sugar

1. Preheat oven to 350°F.

2. Combine cake mix, 1 egg and shortening in bowl. Beat at low speed with electric mixer until crumbs form. Reserve 1 cup. Pat remaining mixture into *ungreased* 13×9-inch pan. Bake 15 minutes or until lightly browned.

3. Combine remaining 2 eggs, granulated sugar, lemon juice, lemon peel, baking powder and salt in bowl. Beat at medium speed with electric mixer until light and foamy. Pour over hot crust; sprinkle with reserved crumb mixture.

4. Bake 15 minutes or until lightly browned. Sprinkle with confectioners' sugar. Cool in pan. Cut into bars.

Makes 30 to 32 bars

Pudding Poke Brownies

- 1 package (19.8 ounces) brownie mix
- 1 1/2 cups cold milk
- 1 package (4-serving size) JELL-O® Instant Pudding & Pie Filling, any flavor

PREPARE and bake brownie mix as directed on package in an 8- or 9-inch square pan. Remove from oven. Immediately poke holes down through brownies to pan at 1-inch intervals with round handle of wooden spoon. (Or poke holes with plastic drinking straw, using turning motion to make large holes.)

POUR milk into large bowl. Add pudding mix. Beat with wire whisk 2 minutes. Quickly pour about 1/2 of the thin pudding mixture evenly over warm brownies into holes. Let remaining pudding mixture stand to thicken slightly. Spoon over top of brownies, swirling to frost brownies.

REFRIGERATE at least 1 hour or until ready to serve.

Makes 16 servings

Lemon Bars

Spicy Oatmeal Raisin Cookies

1 package DUNCAN HINES® Moist Deluxe® Spice Cake Mix
4 egg whites
1 cup uncooked quick-cooking oats (not instant or old-fashioned)
½ cup vegetable oil
½ cup raisins

1. Preheat oven to 350°F. Grease cookie sheets.

2. Combine cake mix, egg whites, oats and oil in large mixing bowl. Beat at low speed with electric mixer until blended. Stir in raisins. Drop by rounded teaspoonfuls onto prepared cookie sheets.

3. Bake 7 to 9 minutes or until lightly browned. Cool 1 minute on cookie sheets. Remove to cooling racks; cool completely.

Makes 4 dozen cookies

Spicy Oatmeal Raisin Cookies

Chocolate Cherry Cookies

1 package (8 ounces) sugar-free low-fat chocolate cake mix
3 tablespoons fat-free (skim) milk
½ teaspoon almond extract
10 maraschino cherries, rinsed, drained and cut into halves
2 tablespoons white chocolate chips
½ teaspoon vegetable oil

1. Preheat oven to 350°F. Spray baking sheets with nonstick cooking spray; set aside.

2. Beat cake mix, milk and almond extract in medium bowl with electric mixer at low speed. Increase speed to medium when mixture looks crumbly; beat 2 minutes or until smooth dough forms. (Dough will be very sticky.)

3. Coat hands with cooking spray. Shape dough into 1-inch balls. Place balls 2½ inches apart on prepared baking sheets. Flatten each ball slightly. Place cherry half in center of each cookie.

4. Bake 8 to 9 minutes or until cookies lose their shininess and tops begin to crack. Do not overbake. Remove to wire racks; cool completely.

5. Heat white chocolate chips and oil in small saucepan over very low heat until chips melt. Drizzle cookies with melted chips. Allow drizzle to harden before serving. *Makes 20 cookies*

Magical Tip

Completely cool all cookies before storing in airtight containers. Store each kind of cookie separately to prevent transfer of flavor and changes in texture.

Enchanting Desserts

Brownie Ice Cream Pie

- 1 package DUNCAN HINES® Chewy Fudge Brownie Mix
- 2 eggs
- ½ cup vegetable oil
- ¼ cup water
- ¾ cup semisweet chocolate chips
- 1 (9-inch) unbaked pastry crust
- 1 (10-ounce) package frozen sweetened sliced strawberries
- Vanilla ice cream

1. Preheat oven to 350°F.

2. Combine brownie mix, eggs, oil and water. Stir with spoon until blended, about 50 strokes. Stir in chips. Spoon into crust. Bake 40 to 45 minutes or until set. Cool. Purée strawberries in food processor. Cut pie into wedges. Serve with ice cream and puréed strawberries. *Makes 8 servings*

Brownie Ice Cream Pie

Individual Cheesecake Cups

Crust

1 package DUNCAN HINES® Moist Deluxe® Yellow or Devil's Food Cake Mix

¼ cup margarine or butter, melted

Cheese Filling

2 packages (8 ounces each) cream cheese, softened

3 eggs

¾ cup sugar

1 teaspoon vanilla extract

Topping

1½ cups dairy sour cream

¼ cup sugar

1 can (21 ounces) cherry pie filling (optional)

1. Preheat oven to 350°F. Place 2½-inch foil or paper liners in 24 muffin cups.

2. For crust, combine cake mix and melted ¼ cup margarine in large bowl. Beat at low speed with electric mixer for 1 minute. Mixture will be crumbly. Divide mixture evenly among muffin cups. Level but do not press.

3. For filling, combine cream cheese, eggs, ¾ cup sugar and vanilla extract in medium bowl. Beat at medium speed with electric mixer until smooth. Spoon evenly into muffin cups. Bake at 350°F for 20 minutes or until set.

4. For topping, combine sour cream and ¼ cup sugar in small bowl. Spoon evenly over cheesecakes. Return to oven for 5 minutes. Cool completely. Garnish each cheesecake with cherry pie filling, if desired. Refrigerate until ready to serve.

Makes 24 servings

Magical Tip

To melt ¼ cup (½ stick) of margarine or butter, place it in a microwavable measuring cup or bowl. Heat at HIGH 50 to 60 seconds.

Individual Cheesecake Cups

Rum and Spumone Layered Torte

1 package (18 to 19 ounces) moist butter recipe yellow cake mix
3 eggs
½ cup butter, softened
⅓ cup plus 2 teaspoons rum, divided
⅓ cup water
1 quart spumone ice cream, softened
1 cup whipping cream
1 tablespoon powdered sugar
Candied cherries
Red and green sugars for decorating (optional)

• Preheat oven to 375°F. Grease and flour 15½×10½×1-inch jelly-roll pan. Combine cake mix, eggs, butter, ⅓ cup rum and water in large bowl. Beat with electric mixer at low speed just until moistened. Beat at high speed 4 minutes. Pour evenly into prepared pan.

• Bake 20 to 25 minutes or until toothpick inserted in center comes out clean. Cool in pan 10 minutes. Turn out of pan onto wire rack; cool completely.

• Cut cake into three 10×5-inch pieces. Place one cake layer on serving plate. Spread with half the softened ice cream. Cover with second cake layer. Spread with remaining ice cream. Place remaining cake layer on top. Gently push down. Wrap cake in plastic wrap and freeze at least 4 hours.

• Just before serving, combine cream, powdered sugar and remaining 2 teaspoons rum in small chilled bowl. Beat at high speed with chilled beaters until stiff peaks form. Remove cake from freezer. Spread thin layer of whipped cream mixture over top of cake. Place star tip in pastry bag; fill with remaining whipped cream mixture. Pipe rosettes around outer top edges of cake. Place cherries in narrow strip down center of cake. Sprinkle colored sugars over rosettes, if desired. Serve immediately.

Makes 12 servings

Rum and Spumone Layered Torte

Hot Fudge Sundae Cake

1 package DUNCAN HINES® Moist Deluxe® Dark Chocolate Fudge Cake Mix
½ gallon brick vanilla ice cream

Fudge Sauce
1 can (12 ounces) evaporated milk
1¼ cups sugar
4 squares (1 ounce each) unsweetened chocolate
¼ cup butter or margarine
1½ teaspoons vanilla extract
¼ teaspoon salt
Whipped cream and maraschino cherries, for garnish

1. Preheat oven to 350°F. Grease and flour 13×9×2-inch pan. Prepare, bake and cool cake following package directions.

2. Remove cake from pan. Split cake in half horizontally. Place bottom layer back in pan. Cut ice cream into even slices and place evenly over bottom cake layer (use all the ice cream). Place remaining cake layer over ice cream. Cover and freeze.

3. For fudge sauce, combine evaporated milk and sugar in medium saucepan. Stir constantly on medium heat until mixture comes to a rolling boil. Boil and stir for 1 minute. Add unsweetened chocolate and stir until melted. Beat over medium heat until smooth. Remove from heat. Stir in butter, vanilla and salt.

4. Cut cake into serving squares. For each serving, place cake square on plate; spoon hot fudge sauce on top. Garnish with whipped cream and maraschino cherry.

Makes 12 to 16 servings

Magical Tip

The hot fudge sauce may be prepared ahead and refrigerated in a tightly sealed jar. Reheat it when you are ready to serve the cake.

Hot Fudge Sundae Cake

Double Berry Layer Cake

1 package DUNCAN HINES® Moist Deluxe® Strawberry Supreme Cake Mix
⅔ cup strawberry jam, divided
2½ cups fresh blueberries, rinsed, drained and divided
1 container (8 ounces) frozen whipped topping, thawed and divided
Fresh strawberry slices, for garnish

1. Preheat oven to 350°F. Lightly grease and flour two 9-inch round cake pans.

2. Prepare, bake and cool cake following package directions for basic recipe.

3. Place one cake layer on serving plate. Spread with ⅓ cup jam. Arrange 1 cup blueberries on jam. Spread half the whipped topping to within ½ inch of cake edge. Place second cake layer on top. Repeat with remaining ⅓ cup jam, 1 cup blueberries and remaining whipped topping. Garnish with strawberry slices and remaining ½ cup blueberries. Refrigerate until ready to serve.

Makes 12 servings

Pumpkin Crunch Cake

1 package (18.25 ounces) yellow cake mix, divided
2 eggs
1⅔ cups LIBBY'S® Pumpkin Pie Mix
2 teaspoons pumpkin pie spice
⅓ cup flaked coconut
¼ cup chopped nuts
3 tablespoons butter or margarine, softened

COMBINE *3 cups* cake mix, eggs, pumpkin pie mix and pumpkin pie spice in large mixer bowl. Beat on low speed until moistened. Beat on medium speed for 2 minutes. Pour into greased 13×9-inch baking pan.

COMBINE *remaining* cake mix, coconut and nuts in small bowl; cut in butter with pastry blender or two knives until mixture is crumbly. Sprinkle over batter.

BAKE in preheated 350°F. oven for 30 to 35 minutes or until wooden pick inserted in center comes out clean. Cool in pan on wire rack. *Makes 20 servings*

Double Berry Layer Cake

Chocolate Chip Cheesecake

1 package DUNCAN HINES® Moist Deluxe Devil's Food Cake Mix
½ cup vegetable oil
3 (8-ounce) packages cream cheese, softened
1½ cups granulated sugar
1 cup sour cream
1½ teaspoons vanilla extract
4 eggs, lightly beaten
¾ cup semisweet mini chocolate chips, divided
1 teaspoon all-purpose flour

1. Preheat oven to 350°F. Grease 10-inch springform pan.

2. Combine cake mix and oil in large bowl. Mix well. Press onto bottom of prepared pan. Bake 22 to 25 minutes or until set. Remove from oven. *Increase oven temperature to 450°F.*

3. Place cream cheese in large mixing bowl. Beat at low speed with electric mixer, adding sugar gradually. Add sour cream and vanilla extract, mixing until blended. Add eggs, mixing only until incorporated. Toss ½ cup chocolate chips with flour. Fold into cream cheese mixture. Pour filling onto crust. Sprinkle with remaining ¼ cup chocolate chips.

4. Bake 5 to 7 minutes. *Reduce oven temperature to 250°F.* Bake 60 to 65 minutes or until set. Loosen cake from side of pan with knife or spatula. Cool completely in pan on cooling rack. Refrigerate until ready to serve. Remove side of pan.

Makes 12 to 16 servings

Magical Tip

To prevent the top of the cheesecake from cracking, place a pan of water on the bottom rack of the oven while the cheesecake is baking.

Chocolate Chip Cheesecake

Strawberry Vanilla Cake

1 package DUNCAN HINES® Moist Deluxe® French Vanilla Cake Mix
1 container DUNCAN HINES® Vanilla Frosting, divided
1/3 cup seedless strawberry jam
Fresh strawberries, for garnish (optional)

1. Preheat oven to 350°F. Lightly grease and flour two 8- or 9-inch round pans.

2. Prepare, bake and cool cakes following package directions for basic recipe.

3. To assemble, place one cake layer on serving plate. Place 1/4 cup Vanilla frosting in small resealable plastic bag. Snip off one corner. Pipe a bead of frosting on top of layer around outer edge. Fill remaining area with strawberry jam. Top with second cake layer. Spread remaining frosting on side and top of cake. Decorate with fresh strawberries, if desired.

Makes 12 to 16 servings

Punch Bowl Party Cake

1 package (18¼ ounces) yellow cake mix plus ingredients to prepare mix
1 package (4-serving size) vanilla flavor instant pudding and pie filling mix plus ingredients to prepare mix
2 cans (21 ounces each) cherry pie filling
1 cup chopped pecans
1 container (12 ounces) frozen whipped topping, thawed

Prepare and bake cake following package directions for 13×9-inch cake; cool. Prepare pudding according to package directions. Crumble ½ of cake into bottom of small punch bowl. Cover with ½ of pudding. Reserve a few cherries from one can of cherry pie filling for garnish. Top pudding with layers of cherry pie filling, nuts and whipped topping. Repeat layers, using remaining cake, pudding and cherry pie filling. Top with remaining nuts, whipped topping and reserved cherries.

Makes 12 servings

Decadent Chocolate Delight

- **1 package chocolate cake mix**
- **8 ounces sour cream**
- **1 cup water**
- **4 eggs**
- **¾ cup vegetable oil**
- **1 package (4-serving size) chocolate flavor instant pudding and pie filling mix**
- **1 cup chocolate chips**
- **Ice cream, any flavor, softened (optional)**

Slow Cooker Directions

• Lightly grease inside of slow cooker.

• Combine cake mix, sour cream, water, eggs and oil in large bowl until well blended. Stir in pudding mix until well blended. Stir in chocolate chips.

• Pour mixture into slow cooker. Cover and cook on LOW 6 to 8 hours or on HIGH 3 to 4 hours. Serve hot or warm with ice cream, if desired.

Makes 12 servings

Decadent Chocolate Delight

Chocolate Angel Food Dessert

1 package DUNCAN HINES® Angel Food Cake Mix
16 large marshmallows
½ cup milk
1 package (11 ounces) milk chocolate chips
1 pint whipping cream
¼ cup semisweet chocolate chips
1½ teaspoons shortening

1. Preheat oven to 375°F. Prepare, bake and cool cake following package directions.

2. Melt marshmallows and milk in heavy saucepan over low heat. Remove from heat; stir in milk chocolate chips until melted. Cool to room temperature. Beat whipping cream in bowl until stiff peaks form. Fold cooled chocolate mixture into whipped cream. Chill until spreading consistency.

3. To assemble, split cake horizontally into 3 even layers. Place 1 cake layer on serving plate. Spread with one-fourth of frosting. Repeat with second layer. Top with third layer. Frost side and top with remaining frosting. Chill.

4. For drizzle, place semisweet chocolate chips and shortening in 1-cup glass measuring cup. Microwave at MEDIUM (50% power) for 1 minute. Stir until smooth. Drizzle melted chocolate around outer top edge of cake, allowing mixture to run down side unevenly. Refrigerate until ready to serve.

Makes 12 to 16 servings

Magical Tip

Angel food cake should be cooled in the pan upside down. An angel food cake pan has three metal feet on which the inverted pan stands for cooling. If you use a tube pan instead, invert the pan on a funnel or narrow-necked bottle.

Chocolate Angel Food Dessert

Chocolate Cherry Torte

- 1 package DUNCAN HINES® Moist Deluxe® Devil's Food Cake Mix
- 1 can (21 ounces) cherry pie filling
- 1/4 teaspoon almond extract
- 1 container (8 ounces) frozen whipped topping, thawed and divided
- 1/4 cup toasted sliced almonds, for garnish

1. Preheat oven to 350°F. Lightly grease and flour two 9-inch round cake pans.

2. Prepare, bake and cool cake following package directions for basic recipe. Combine cherry pie filling and almond extract in small bowl. Stir until blended.

3. To assemble, place one cake layer on serving plate. Spread with 1 cup whipped topping, then half the cherry pie filling mixture. Top with second cake layer. Spread remaining pie filling to within 1 1/2 inches of cake edge. Decorate cake edge with remaining whipped topping. Garnish with sliced almonds.

Makes 12 to 16 servings

Pistachio Pudding Cake

- 1 package (2-layer size) yellow cake mix*
- 1 package (4-serving size) JELL-O® Pistachio Flavor Instant Pudding & Pie Filling
- 4 eggs
- 1 1/4 cups water*
- 1/4 cup oil
- 1/2 teaspoon almond extract
- 7 drops green food coloring (optional)
- Powdered sugar

**Or use cake mix with pudding in the mix and reduce water to 1 cup.*

HEAT oven to 350°F.

PLACE all ingredients except powdered sugar in large bowl. Beat with electric mixer on low speed just to moisten. Beat on medium speed 4 minutes. Pour into greased and floured 10-inch fluted tube pan.

BAKE 50 to 55 minutes or until toothpick inserted in center comes out clean.

REMOVE cake from oven. Cool 15 minutes; remove from pan. Cool completely on wire rack. Dust with powdered sugar.

Makes 12 servings

• Acknowledgments •

The publisher would like to thank the companies and organizations listed below for the use of their recipes and photographs in this publication.

Cherry Marketing Institute

Dole Food Company, Inc.

Duncan Hines® and Moist Deluxe®
are registered trademarks of Aurora Foods Inc.

Eagle® Brand

Hershey Foods Corporation

Kraft Foods Holdings

©Mars, Inc. 2001

Nabisco Biscuit and Snack Division

Nestlé USA, Inc.

OREO® Chocolate Sandwich Cookies

Reynolds Consumer Products,
A Business of Alcoa Inc.

Unilever Bestfoods North America

• Index •

• Index •